WORLD'S FASTEST
WATERCRAFT

WWW.APEXEDITIONS.COM

Copyright © 2022 by Apex Editions, Mendota Heights, MN 55120. All rights reserved. No part of this book may be reproduced or utilized in any form or by any means without written permission from the publisher.

Apex is distributed by North Star Editions:
sales@northstareditions.com | 888-417-0195

Produced for Apex by Red Line Editorial.

Photographs ©: Albert Wilson/Alamy, cover, 1; Keystone Pictures USA/Zuma Press/Alamy, 4–5; Shutterstock Images, 6–7, 12, 16–17, 18–19, 20, 21, 24–25, 27, 29; Reed Saxon/AP Images, 8–9; Detroit Publishing Company/Library of Congress, 10–11; Ajax News & Feature Service/Alamy, 13; AP Images, 14, 15; Jonathan Torgovnik/Reportage/Getty Images News/ Getty Images, 22–23; Colin Underhill/Alamy, 26

Library of Congress Control Number: 2021918551

ISBN
978-1-63738-175-5 (hardcover)
978-1-63738-211-0 (paperback)
978-1-63738-279-0 (ebook pdf)
978-1-63738-247-9 (hosted ebook)

Printed in the United States of America
Mankato, MN
012022

NOTE TO PARENTS AND EDUCATORS

Apex books are designed to build literacy skills in striving readers. Exciting, high-interest content attracts and holds readers' attention. The text is carefully leveled to allow students to achieve success quickly. Additional features, such as bolded glossary words for difficult terms, help build comprehension.

TABLE OF CONTENTS

JET SPEED

A white boat zooms across the water. A man sits in its small cockpit. He's strapped in like the pilot of an airplane. Behind him, jet engines roar. They send the boat racing forward.

In 2021, *Spirit of Australia* had been the fastest boat in the world for 43 years.

As the boat gains speed, most of its **hull** lifts above of the water. **Sponsons** on the sides help keep it stable.

The front ends of racing boats tip up at high speeds. This helps the boats skim quickly across the water.

HYDROPLANES

Many fast boats are hydroplanes. These boats have flat bottoms. Only parts of their hulls touch the water. The rest lifts up. This helps the boats go faster.

The boat goes just over 317 miles per hour (510 km/h). It's a new world record!

Ken Warby set the water speed record in 1978. As of 2021, no one had beaten it.

In 1997, Ken Warby posed with a photo of *Spirit of Australia.*

CHAPTER 2

MOTORBOAT HISTORY

F or many years, most boats got power from wind, oars, or paddles. But in the 1900s, people began making motorboats. They used motors based on car engines.

A motorboat rides the waters of Detroit, Michigan, in the early 1900s.

Boats with outboard motors remain common today.

Outboard motors became common in the 1910s. In the 1940s, people began making hulls from fiberglass. This material is lighter than wood or metal.

HULL SHAPE

Some boat hulls push lots of water out of the way. Flatter hulls push against less water. Boats that have them tend to go faster.

In 1939, the hydroplane *Bluebird II* set the water speed record of 142 miles per hour (229 km/h).

These improvements led to greater speeds. In 1962, *Miss US 1* became the first boat to reach 200 miles per hour (322 km/h).

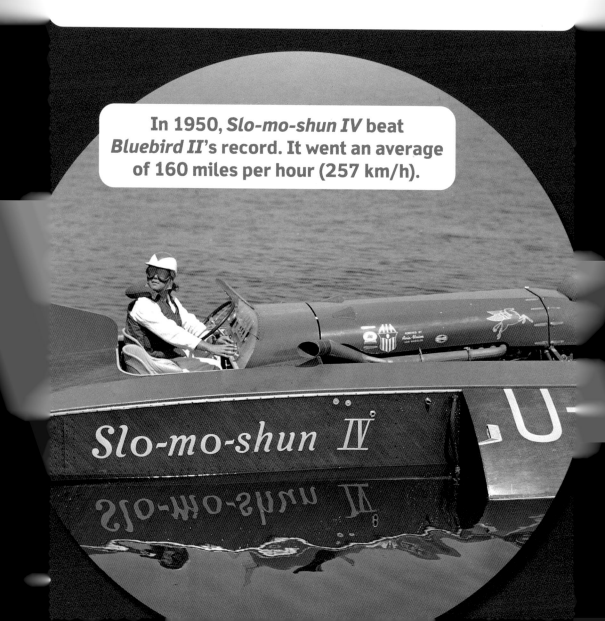

In 1950, *Slo-mo-shun IV* beat *Bluebird II*'s record. It went an average of 160 miles per hour (257 km/h).

In 1955, Donald Malcolm Campbell became the first person to successfully pilot a jet-propelled boat.

Today, many of the fastest boats use inboard motors.

CHAPTER 3

FASTEST SPEEDBOATS

As of 2021, Ken Warby's boat is still the fastest. *Bluebird K7* is second. It went 276 miles per hour (444 km/h) in 1964.

Like Ken Warby's *Spirit of Australia*, *Bluebird K7* used jet engines.

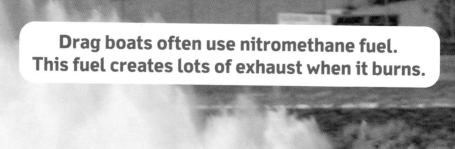

Drag boats often use nitromethane fuel. This fuel creates lots of exhaust when it burns.

Problem Child takes third place. It can go 262 miles per hour (422 km/h). This drag boat's huge engine creates 8,000 **horsepower**.

Problem Child can reach its top speed in 3.5 seconds.

Fourth place goes to the Mystic C5000. This type of powerboat can go 250 miles per hour (402 km/h). Its fuel tank holds 600 gallons (2,271 L) of fuel.

Miss *GEICO* is a famous C5000. This powerboat has won many racing world championships.

Personal watercraft are small vehicles, such as jet skis. Most go just over 65 miles per hour (105 km/h).

PWC SPEED

In 2017, Uva Perez set the speed record for personal watercraft (PWC). He rode a **turbocharged** Yamaha FZR WaveRunner. It went 127 miles per hour (204 km/h).

CHAPTER 4

OTHER WATERCRAFT

In 2021, *Vestas Sailrocket 2* held the speed-sailing record. This boat went 75 miles per hour (121 km/h) in 2012.

Vestas Sailrocket 2 has a small, tilted hull and a huge sail.

Some superfast sailboats have three hulls. These boats are called trimarans.

Newer boats could go even faster. One is pulled by a kite. Another mostly floats above water. But it has a small underwater **foil**.

UNDERWATER BUBBLES

As a boat moves, bubbles form in the water around it. When these bubbles pop, they produce **shock waves**. To prevent damage, scientists look for designs that help control these bubbles.

The fastest human-powered watercraft is a type of **hydrofoil**. In 1991, it went 21 miles per hour (34 km/h). As of 2021, no one had broken that record.

One human-powered hydrofoil is the AquaSk

A hydrofoil is part boat and part plane.

In 2021, *Foners* was the fastest yacht. It could go about 80 miles per hour (129 km/h).

COMPREHENSION QUESTIONS

Write your answers on a separate piece of paper.

1. Write a sentence describing the main ideas from Chapter 2.

2. Would you want to try setting a world record for speed? If so, what record would you want to set? If not, why?

3. What is the name for a boat with a flat bottom that lifts partly out of the water at high speeds?

    A. a hydroplane

    B. a yacht

    C. a sponson

4. Why would pushing against less water help boats with flat hulls go faster?

    A. Pushing against water slows boats down.

    B. Pushing against water helps boats turn.

    C. Pushing against water takes less energy.

5. What does **material** mean in this book?

*In the 1940s, people began making hulls from fiberglass. This **material** is lighter than wood or metal.*

    A. something used for cooking
    B. something used for building
    C. something that doesn't actually exist

6. What does **produce** mean in this book?

*As a boat moves, bubbles form in the water around it. When these bubbles pop, they **produce** shock waves.*

    A. fruits and vegetables
    B. to make or cause
    C. to ignore

Answer key on page 32.

GLOSSARY

foil
A metal plate or fin that attaches to a boat so the boat's hull will lift out of the water at fast speeds.

horsepower
A unit that measures the power of engines and motors. A standard car engine usually has about 200 horsepower.

hull
The main part of a ship or boat.

hydrofoil
A type of watercraft with a hull that can lift completely above water at high speeds.

inboard motors
Engines that are placed inside a boat's body.

outboard motors
Engines that attach to the outside of a boat, usually at the back.

shock waves
Waves of fast-moving air or water that can damage the things they hit.

sponsons
Parts that stick out from a vehicle's sides to help it balance.

turbocharged
Given extra parts to make the engine work better or faster.

TO LEARN MORE

BOOKS

Hamilton, S. L. *The World's Fastest Boats*. Minneapolis: Abdo Publishing, 2021.

Klepeis, Alicia Z. *Superfast Boats*. Minneapolis: Jump!, 2022.

Skene, Rona. *Amazing Vehicles*. New York: DK Publishing, 2019.

ONLINE RESOURCES

Visit **www.apexeditions.com** to find links and resources related to this title.

ABOUT THE AUTHOR

Brienna Rossiter is a writer and editor who lives in Minnesota. She enjoys reading about animals and science.

INDEX

Answer Key:
1. Answers will vary; 2. Answers will vary; 3. A; 4. A; 5. B; 6. B